Original title:
Bruised but Strong

Copyright © 2024 Swan Charm
All rights reserved.

Author: Sara Säde
ISBN HARDBACK: 978-9916-79-006-9
ISBN PAPERBACK: 978-9916-79-007-6
ISBN EBOOK: 978-9916-79-008-3

The Spirit that Endures

In shadows deep, we find our light,
As stars emerge in the dark of night.
Whispers carry tales of grace,
In every heart, a sacred place.

Through storms that rage and tempests wild,
The spirit soft, yet fierce as a child.
With every tear that falls in vain,
Resilience blooms amidst the pain.

Mountains rise, and valleys low,
In every journey, our spirits grow.
With open arms, we face the fight,
Guided by love, we seek the bright.

In moments lost, in battles fought,
A tapestry of lessons taught.
Each heartbeat sings of hope anew,
A testament to what we do.

So let us dance in life's embrace,
With every step, we find our place.
Together strong, our voices blend,
In unity, our spirits mend.

The Pulse of Defiance

In shadows deep, we strive and fight,
Echoes of courage, igniting the night.
Voices together, a roaring sound,
We rise like flames from the ashes, unbound.

Hearts beating strong, a resolute beat,
Against the silence, we refuse defeat.
Chains may bind, but spirits soar,
With each pulse of defiance, we'll roar.

Mending the Shattered

Fragments of dreams lie scattered wide,
Yet hope remains, a gentle guide.
Piece by piece, we start to mend,
Healing the wounds, embracing the bend.

Tender hands weave a tapestry bright,
Colors of courage in the soft light.
From brokenness, beauty will rise,
In every scar, a story lies.

In the Face of the Tempest

Winds howl fierce, a darkened sky,
Yet we stand firm, never to cry.
Roots run deep, we won't be swayed,
In the face of the tempest, we're unafraid.

Storms may rage, the floods may swell,
But in our hearts, a tale to tell.
Together we rise, against all odds,
In unity's strength, we find the gods.

Unearthing Inner Fortitude

Deep within, a light does glow,
A well of strength that we can show.
Unveil the power, unleashed it will be,
For courage lives in the depths of the sea.

With every challenge, we must ignite,
A spark of defiance, a burning light.
In trials faced, we find our role,
Unearthing the fortitude of the soul.

Tenderness of Tenacity

In quiet pleas of strength we find,
A gentle grip, a heart aligned.
The storms may howl, yet we stand tall,
With every tear, a brave new call.

Through shadows cast by doubt and fear,
In soft embrace, the visions clear.
For every fall, we rise anew,
With tenderness, we push on through.

Strength Beneath the Surface

Beneath the calm, the currents churn,
A hidden fire, where passions burn.
In silent depths, the courage sleeps,
A strength that wakes, a promise keeps.

With echoes of the battles fought,
The surface masks what can't be taught.
Yet through the waves, a spirit bold,
Unseen, it weaves a tale untold.

A Symphony of Scars

Each scar a note, a story played,
In symphony, our strength displayed.
With melodies of pain and grace,
We dance to life, we find our place.

The chords are deep, the harmony,
A testament to what can be.
In every crack, a light shines through,
A song of hope, forever true.

The Heart's Untold Stories

In whispered breaths, the heart will speak,
Of love and loss, of strong and weak.
Beneath the skin, a world resides,
With every beat, a truth abides.

The tales of joy, the shadows cast,
A tapestry of futures past.
In silence held, the truths will swell,
In every thump, a wish to tell.

The Pulse of Perseverance

In shadows deep, we rise anew,
With every step, the courage grew.
A heartbeat strong, we stand and fight,
Determined souls, we seek the light.

With grit and grace, we hold our ground,
Through storms that toss, we will rebound.
Each challenge faced, we learn and thrive,
Our spirits bold, we stay alive.

A whisper soft, yet loud and clear,
The dreams we chase, we will draw near.
With every fall, we find our way,
In perseverance, we choose our day.

The flame within, it flickers bright,
Igniting hope in darkest night.
With lustrous hearts, we march ahead,
In paths of strength, our fears are shed.

For in this journey, we belong,
Each heartbeat echoes like a song.
Together strong, we'll pave the road,
The pulse of life, our shared abode.

Silent Roars of Strength

In quietude, the lions roar,
Their hearts alive, forever soar.
With silent strength, they tread the land,
In resolute, they make a stand.

Threads of courage weave the night,
In subtle ways, they spark the light.
Soft whispers hold the force within,
The battle starts, the fight begins.

Each breath a pulse that strikes the air,
In stillness grand, they lay their prayer.
Voices strong, protect the weak,
In unity, the strong we seek.

Together in the shadows cast,
Their echo leads, the die is cast.
For silent roars in hearts so true,
Reveal the strength that lives in you.

In steadfast grace, they move with pride,
Unseen but felt, they turn the tide.
With every step, new paths we find,
In silent roars, we're intertwined.

Emblem of Survival

In wilderness where shadows dwell,
An emblem grows, a tale to tell.
Through thorns and brambles, fierce we stride,
In the face of odds, we won't subside.

With eyes like stars, we seek the way,
In every night, we forge the day.
Resilience carved on borrowed time,
An anthem born from pain and rhyme.

Roots entwined in solid ground,
From ashes rise, our voice profound.
In storms and trials, we are reborn,
An emblem bright of hope, not scorn.

Together strong, we break the chains,
In unity, we share the pains.
A tapestry of scars to show,
An emblem bold, we choose to glow.

Through fire and rain, we stand as one,
In every challenge, love has won.
The emblem shines, a symbol clear,
Of survival's heart, we persevere.

From Darkness, a Flicker

In shadows deep, hope whispers low,
A spark ignites where no light flows.
Amidst despair, a chance to dream,
A flicker shines, a gentle beam.

Faint glimmers dance, a promise sweet,
As weary hearts refuse defeat.
From silent depths where sorrows dwell,
Emerges strength, a tale to tell.

Through winding paths, the spirit leads,
A guiding star when courage bleeds.
In darkest nights, we find our way,
With every dawn, a brand new day.

Together we rise, hand in hand,
Reaching for light, together we stand.
From darkness vast, our voices strong,
Creating hope, where we belong.

So hold on tight, let shadows fade,
In every heart, a fierce crusade.
We are the flickers, fierce and bright,
Turning the dark to brilliant light.

The Power of Perseverance

In restless nights, we face our fears,
Through blood and sweat, we dry our tears.
Each setback shapes our steadfast hearts,
Uniting souls, as strength imparts.

With every trial, a lesson learned,
Through stormy skies, our passions burned.
Resilience rises, a flame renewed,
We journey forth, with hope imbued.

Though paths may twist, and shadows loom,
In depths of pain, we find our bloom.
For every stumble, we stand tall,
The power within, it conquers all.

So here we strive, through thick and thin,
With grit and grace, we fight and win.
For every battle, we share the load,
Together, we forge a brighter road.

Embrace the grind, for strength we gain,
In perseverance, we'll break each chain.
United, we climb, we will ascend,
In every heartbeat, we rise, transcend.

Grounded in Grace

In quiet moments, we embrace,
The gentle touch of timeless grace.
In breaths of peace, our spirits soar,
With every heartbeat, we want more.

Through trials faced, we find our way,
In kindness shared, we choose to stay.
The earth beneath, so strong, so true,
In roots of love, we begin anew.

As seasons shift, and winds may change,
In solitude, we learn, exchange.
With open hearts, we face the dawn,
In grace, united, we press on.

The beauty lies in simple things,
In laughter shared, the joy it brings.
For in each moment, we can find,
The strength to heal, a life unlined.

So walk with me, through paths unknown,
Together, we'll make our spirits grown.
With every step, in time and space,
We blossom bright, grounded in grace.

Phoenix from the Fragments

From ashes scattered, hope will rise,
A phoenix born, beneath the skies.
In each burnt piece, a story lies,
A tale of strength that never dies.

Through darkest nights, we learn to soar,
With wings of fire, we find the door.
Amidst the shatters, we reclaim,
The spark within, igniting flame.

Though storms may rage, and fears abound,
In fractured dreams, new paths are found.
We gather pieces, stitch them well,
In every shard, a tale to tell.

Resilient heart, with fierce intent,
To rise anew, we're heaven-sent.
For in our depths, the light we find,
Unveiling purpose, heart and mind.

So watch us rise, from broken ground,
With every beat, new hopes unbound.
A phoenix reigns, its spirit grand,
From fragments lost, we take a stand.

Strength in the Silence

In quiet moments, spirits rise,
Resilience whispers, no need for cries.
Beneath the weight of all we bear,
A silent strength, beyond compare.

With every breath, we find our ground,
Glimmers of hope in silence found.
Through darkest nights, our hearts will strive,
In the stillness, we come alive.

Embracing shadows, we hold fast,
Memories linger, echoes cast.
In solitude, we learn to heal,
The strength in silence begins to feel.

Through trials faced, we stand so tall,
In muted grace, we rise from the fall.
Each unspoken word, a step towards light,
In the silence, we find our fight.

So trust the quiet, let it speak,
In every heart, it's solace we seek.
For in the silence, we'll find our way,
To brighter dawns, through night and day.

Echoes of Endurance

Across the plains, our stories roam,
Each echo carries a sense of home.
Through battles fought, we stand as one,
The spirit of endurance, never done.

In every heart, a fire burns bright,
Guiding us through the endless night.
With every setback, we rise again,
An echo of strength, an enduring refrain.

Through storms we've weathered, we've grown bold,
In moments of silence, our truths unfold.
With every step, we break the chain,
The echoes of endurance will ever remain.

Together we stand, through thick and thin,
Each voice a reminder, we will win.
The path may twist, the road may bend,
In the echoes of hope, we find our friends.

So hear the whispers, let them guide,
In the echoes, we take our stride.
Through trials faced, our courage sings,
In the heart of endurance, life springs.

Torn but Triumphant

Like petals scattered in the breeze,
We rise from chaos, hearts at ease.
Though torn apart by storms we face,
In the struggle, we find grace.

With wounds that speak of battles fought,
In every challenge, a lesson taught.
Though weary limbs may need to rest,
In the brokenness, we are blessed.

Each scar a badge of courage worn,
From every tear, a new hope is born.
Through the cracks, the light shines through,
Torn but triumphant, we are renewed.

So let the winds of change unfold,
Embrace the stories yet untold.
For in our hearts, the strength to stand,
With every heartbeat, we make our stand.

Torn but triumphant, we rise each day,
With resilience guiding, come what may.
From shattered dreams, we'll build anew,
In the journey, our spirits grew.

The Art of Survival

In the dance of life, we learn to adapt,
Crafting our path, where shadows have mapped.
With each heartbeat, we find our way,
In the art of survival, we choose to stay.

Through the storms that seek to invade,
We weave our strength, unafraid.
Colors of hope brush the gray,
In every struggle, we find our sway.

With eyes wide open, we gather the light,
From moments of darkness, we soar to new heights.
Each breath a canvas, each choice a stroke,
In the art of survival, we are awoke.

We find the beauty in every tear,
In laughter and joy, we conquer fear.
Turning the pages of life's grand tale,
In the art of survival, we shall prevail.

So cherish the journey, embrace the fight,
With every dawn, we illuminate the night.
Together we stand, in this cosmic swirl,
In the art of survival, we paint our world.

Strength Whispers Softly

In shadows deep, a quiet might,
Resilience blooms in silent night.
Each gentle breath, a pulse of grace,
Courage found in heart's embrace.

Whispers weave through tiresome hours,
Soft as petals, brave as flowers.
Strength is forged as soft winds blow,
In whispered tales that only grow.

Beneath the weight of silent fears,
Strength whispers softly through the years.
In stillness, empires rise and fall,
Yet whispers, they can conquer all.

Embrace the truth, let shadows fade,
In every heartbeat, strength is made.
Feel the power in gentle sighs,
For in the quiet, greatness lies.

Healing in the Hush

A tender heart in silent prayer,
Finds healing in the tranquil air.
Whispers dance like autumn leaves,
In quiet moments, the spirit weaves.

Soft the touch of morning light,
Bringing solace, pure and bright.
In the hush, the soul can mend,
Time a gentle, faithful friend.

Echoes fade, the noise grows dim,
In solitude, the heart can swim.
With each breath, the past subsides,
In healing waters, peace abides.

Listen close to what's unseen,
In silence lies the in-between.
Hope is born where whispers grow,
Healing gifts from deep below.

The Courage to Emerge

From depths of fear, a spark ignites,
The courage found in darkest nights.
With trembling hands, dreams take their flight,
Emerging into morning light.

Old shells shatter, new paths unfold,
A story forged, brave and bold.
Each step a dance, a leap, a chance,
In strength of heart, we find romance.

With whispers soft, the heart will say,
"Fear not the storms, you'll find your way."
So rise, dear soul, embrace your fate,
For in the struggle, love awaits.

Trust the journey, let it flow,
There's courage where the wild winds blow.
In every scar, the tale persists,
The courage to emerge, it exists.

When Silence Speaks Volumes

In quiet halls where shadows play,
The heart speaks loud in its own way.
Each sigh, a word; each glance, a thought,
In silence, truths are dearly sought.

The pause that holds the weight of time,
In hushed tones, we learn to chime.
When voices fade, and echoes cease,
In silence, weary souls find peace.

Look deep within, the silence shouts,
Revealing fears and longing doubts.
Within the stillness, stories thrive,
Where whispering souls are kept alive.

Listen close to what's unsaid,
In quiet realms, our hearts are led.
When silence speaks, it speaks for all,
A gentle strength, a righteous call.

Strength Stitched in Silence

In shadows where whispers dwell,
Quiet strength begins to swell.
Threads of courage, woven tight,
A tapestry forged in the night.

Silent battles, unseen scars,
Fighting demons, reaching stars.
With every tear, a stitch of grace,
Building fortitude in space.

The heart beats with gentle might,
In solitude, it takes its flight.
From quietude, a power grows,
In the silence, one truly knows.

Through every challenge, still we rise,
With steadfast hearts and open skies.
In the hush, our strength we find,
A fusion of body, soul, and mind.

Bound by the silence, not by fate,
We stitch our scars, we cultivate.
With every thread, our hope shines bright,
In silence, we embrace the fight.

Tender Toughness

A gentle heart with iron will,
In softest moments, strength can spill.
A flower blooms with roots so deep,
In every tear, a promise keep.

Through storms that try to bend the bold,
Comes the tender, fierce, and hold.
Resilience wrapped in fragile skin,
In every loss, a chance to win.

With kindness as its guiding light,
Toughness thrives in day and night.
In laughter shared, in sorrows known,
From life's harsh winds, we have grown.

Every bruise tells a story vast,
In every struggle, shadows cast.
Yet in the quiet of the soul,
Tenderness makes the spirit whole.

So let the world both test and try,
We'll reach for stars in the calming sky.
For in our hearts, a truth prevails,
Tender toughness never fails.

The Quiet Roar Within

In stillness, a tempest brews,
A silent force, which cannot lose.
Whispers echo, strong and clear,
In every heartbeat, courage near.

Beneath the calm, the fire glows,
A strength that only the spirit knows.
In moments lost, where shadows play,
Resilience thrives in the light of day.

Each challenge met with grace and poise,
Unseen, but felt in the heart's noise.
From depths of silence, we arise,
With quiet roars, we touch the skies.

In quiet times, we train, prepare,
Gather power with utmost care.
Through trials faced and voices hushed,
The spirit roars, the silence flushed.

Embrace the stillness, embrace the storm,
Finding strength in every form.
The quiet roar, a dance divine,
A symphony in every line.

Unfolding from Adversity

Through cracks, the light begins to creep,
From the depths we've fought to keep.
In every challenge, a lesson learned,
Through every heartache, wisdom burned.

With roots that dig in rocky soil,
Emerging strength through pain and toil.
From brokenness, we rise anew,
Unfolding courage in every hue.

When storms rage high, we hold our ground,
In the chaos, resilience found.
Through jagged edges, beauty grows,
In adversity, the spirit knows.

Each scar a badge, each bruise a tale,
In trials faced, we shall not pale.
From ashes rise, we spread our wings,
Finding freedom that hardship brings.

So when the shadows try to sway,
Remember the strength we've learned to play.
Through every trial, we shall ascend,
Unfolding our beauty, we are not end.

Glimmers in the Grit

In the depths where shadows dwell,
Hope whispers soft, casts its spell.
Beneath the weight, we still shall rise,
Finding beauty in the cries.

Through the storms, our spirits strive,
Each scar a mark, a sign we thrive.
Glimmers shine from within the grime,
Resilience blooms, transcending time.

With every misstep, we learn anew,
In the struggle, we find our view.
A tapestry woven from pain and grace,
Even in darkness, we find our place.

Casting fears like stones to send,
Emerging strong, we shall not bend.
Through every trial, we find a light,
Glimmers in the grit, shining bright.

Embrace the journey, let it unfold,
In every heart, a tale of gold.
Together we rise, united and bold,
In the grit of life, our stories told.

The Beauty of Battle Wounds

Each battle fought, a tale to share,
In scars we wear, a life laid bare.
A canvas etched with lessons learned,
In every wound, our passion burned.

Through the struggles, we find our grace,
In the rubble, we find our place.
Courage blooms where once was pain,
Strength is forged through every strain.

With every stumble, the heart expands,
Dancing with fate, we take our stands.
The beauty lies in how we heal,
Embracing all the wounds we feel.

Victory crowned with broken skin,
A testament to where we've been.
In the seams of life, we find our thread,
The beauty of wounds, where hopes are fed.

From ashes rise, our spirits soar,
Grateful for what we've had to endure.
In each battle, a lesson grows,
The beauty of wounds forever glows.

A Symphony of Survival

In the silence, we hear the sound,
Of hearts that rise from the underground.
Through trials faced, we gather near,
In each note played, our truth is clear.

Echoes of pain, they dance with grace,
Rhythms of life, we embrace the chase.
A symphony built from every fall,
Together we rise, we hear the call.

With strength and hope, we compose our song,
Each lyric woven, where we belong.
Verses of struggle, harmonies of cheer,
A symphony of survival, loud and clear.

When darkness calls and fear draws near,
In unity, we conquer the sheer.
Through every storm, we'll find our way,
In each heartbeat, we choose to stay.

Together we'll play on through the night,
In every challenge, we find our light.
Crafted with love, a score divine,
A symphony of survival, our hearts entwine.

Heartbeats of the Unbroken

In the silence, a heart beats strong,
Each pulse a reminder that we belong.
Through the trials, we face with pride,
In the rhythm of life, we'll not hide.

With every heartbeat, we find our way,
Rising again, come what may.
Echoes of dreams not yet fulfilled,
In the depths, our spirits distilled.

Life's melody plays a fierce refrain,
From ashes we rise, time and again.
In the dance of resilience, we embrace,
Heartbeats of the unbroken, our grace.

Though storms may rage and shadows loom,
In unity, we find our bloom.
Together we march, our voices raised,
In solidarity, we are praised.

For every heartbeat is a fight, a vow,
To cherish the journey and the now.
In every moment, love's truth spoken,
We are the heartbeat of the unbroken.

The Grace of a Stumble

In the dance of chance we sway,
Falling softly, finding our way.
Each misstep a lesson clear,
In the laughter, we lose our fear.

Through the grass, we learn to climb,
With every bruise, we gain in time.
The ground may rise as we descend,
Yet beauty blooms where breaks transcend.

Stars appear in twilight's splash,
Beneath our feet, the silence crashes.
In every tumble, grace reveals,
A path of hearts, a dance that heals.

Let the stumble not be the end,
For in the fall, we learn to mend.
With open arms, we embrace the rise,
In grace, we find our place, our skies.

Phoenix in the Night

From the ashes, fire takes flight,
Wings of ember, burning bright.
Through the dark, a glow shall shine,
A whispered hope, a fate divine.

In shadows deep, the spirit stirs,
With every tear, rebirth occurs.
The night may hold its daunting chill,
But courage kindles, strong and still.

A dance of flames against the dusk,
From depths of loss, arise we must.
The heart ignites, refuse the fright,
For in the struggle, we find our light.

Above the ruins, brightness soars,
With every beat, the spirit roars.
So let the fire guide your way,
In darkness deep, the phoenix stays.

Roots of Resilience

Beneath the surface, strength awaits,
In quiet soil, the heart creates.
With every storm, the roots grow deep,
Through trials faced, our spirits leap.

Branches swaying, reaching high,
Underneath, the roots comply.
Nurtured well by pain and care,
In every whisper, life lays bare.

Seasons change, the winds will blow,
But in the quiet, resilience flows.
Through shadowed paths and sunlit days,
The roots will guide in hidden ways.

With gentle strength, we learn to stand,
Embracing life with open hand.
In every challenge, we shall thrive,
For in our roots, we are alive.

Shadows Cast by Light

In twilight's glow, the shadows dance,
Painting stories with each glance.
Where light meets dark, the day exudes,
The magic woven in realitudes.

In the depths where whispers fade,
Shadows form a soft cascade.
In every corner where dreams spill,
Light and dark, a gentle thrill.

With every heartbeat, echoes play,
Casting forms that lead the way.
In the interplay of dusk and dawn,
We find the strength to carry on.

Let shadows teach their silent art,
For in the dark, we find our heart.
With every glimmer, hope ignites,
In shadows cast, we discover lights.

The Heart that Refuses to Yield

In shadows deep, the heart beats strong,
Against the tide, it sings along.
Through storms that rage and fears that loom,
It finds a way to break the gloom.

Each bruise a mark, each tear a tale,
A journey forged where others fail.
With every pulse, it learns to rise,
A flame within that never dies.

When whispers doubt and shadows creep,
The heart holds firm, its promise steep.
It knows the path, though rough it may be,
In every crack, it finds the key.

So let the world toss, let it turn,
The heart will fight, the fire will burn.
For in its core, resilience lies,
Against the dark, it ever tries.

And when the night seems ever long,
This heart returns, forever strong.
It beats for dreams, it beats for light,
With every sound, it claims its right.

Holding On to Dreams

In whispers soft, the dreams take flight,
They paint the skies with colors bright.
A gentle hope in every heart,
That pulls us close, won't drift apart.

Through winding roads and nights of doubt,
The dreams we hold, they scream and shout.
Against the noise, they sing their song,
A melody that keeps us strong.

With every step, we chase the dawn,
In moments brave, we carry on.
Those visions clear, like stars they gleam,
In every heart, lives the dream.

For in the struggle, joy will bloom,
As we embrace, dispelling gloom.
The dreams we cherish, fiercely bright,
Illuminate our darkest night.

So hold them tight, those precious things,
For in their grasp, the spirit sings.
A world awaits, with arms spread wide,
Embrace those dreams, let love be your guide.

In the Echo Chamber of Pain

In silence thick, the echoes lie,
A chamber dark where sorrows sigh.
Each whisper lingers, haunting still,
Yet through the shadows, I find my will.

Each memory, a stone I carry,
A weight of hours, at times quite scary.
But in this space, I learn to cope,
To weave from pain a thread of hope.

Through every tear, a lesson's born,
In jagged edges, I am worn.
Yet still I rise, each breath a spark,
In this dark place, I leave my mark.

For pain, though heavy, teaches grace,
And in its depths, I find my place.
Resilience blooms in hardened soil,
From fractured roots, my heart to toil.

So let the echoes serenade,
Each note a guide through the cascade.
In the silence, strength will reign,
I'll forge a path beyond the pain.

Resilience: A Quiet Revolution

In stillness formed, a force awakens,
A quiet strength where hope is taken.
With every heartbeat, soft yet bold,
It tells a tale of dreams retold.

Through whispered winds and gentle rain,
Resilience grows from heartache's chain.
In every struggle, a quiet roar,
A revolution at the core.

With steadfast steps, we change the game,
Through shadows cast, we stoke the flame.
For every fall, we rise anew,
A testament to what is true.

In unity, we stand, we fight,
To break the dawn and claim the light.
A revolution born of grace,
Each soul a spark, each heart a place.

So let us rise, undaunted, free,
In echoes strong, our history.
With quiet power, we will prevail,
A resilience deep, beyond the pale.

Fragments of a Warrior's Soul

In shadows deep, the battles rage,
A heart of steel, yet bruised by age.
Each scar a tale, time's cruel gift,
In silent nights, the spirits lift.

With sword in hand, I stand my ground,
Through whispered fears, my strength is found.
The echoes of the past still call,
But through the fire, I will not fall.

The warrior's path is lined with pain,
Yet through the storm, there's much to gain.
I carry hope like armor strong,
In every breath, I sing my song.

The fragments mend, though worn and torn,
A tapestry of battles sworn.
With every step, I rise anew,
A testament to all I've been through.

With courage bright, I face the dawn,
For in my heart, the fight goes on.
I'll forge ahead, my spirit free,
Fragments combined to form the me.

Within the Cracks of Me

In quiet depths, shadows pool,
Where light once danced, now barely cool.
Within the cracks, the sorrows seep,
In whispered thoughts, the heart must weep.

I gather pieces, scattered wide,
Yet still, they shimmer, beauty's guide.
A mosaic of grief, love, and grace,
In each small flaw, my truth I face.

The wounds will heal, though deep they go,
From every crack, new hope will grow.
With patience soft, the light will break,
In every fissure, dreams awake.

Familiar ghosts, they come to play,
Remind me of the price I pay.
But in the cracks, I learn to see,
The strength that lives inside of me.

So let the light infiltrate the dark,
For every crack holds a hidden spark.
A tapestry woven, fragile yet bright,
Within the cracks, I find my light.

Rise from Ashen Dreams

From whispered embers, hope ignites,
In the stillness of the night.
Ashen dreams fall like the rain,
Yet from the ruin, I'll rise again.

A phoenix call beyond the pain,
Each tear a drop, an old refrain.
Through shadows wrapped in soft despair,
I'll chase the dawn with tender care.

The past may scorch, the flames may bite,
But from the gray, I seek the light.
With every sigh, the ashes shift,
Transforming grief into a gift.

I breathe anew, the air is sweet,
With every beat, my heart's retreat.
I'll soar above the whispers grim,
In every loss, I find my hymn.

So rise with me from dreams once torn,
Embrace the light, a new day's born.
From ashen paths, my spirit beams,
In faithful flight, I rise from dreams.

Unyielding Through the Storm

The winds may howl, the skies may weep,
Yet in my soul, a promise deep.
With every gust, I find my place,
Unyielding heart in nature's embrace.

The thunder rolls, the shadows creep,
But through the noise, I will not sleep.
A beacon bright within the fray,
I stand my ground, come what may.

Resilience flows like rivers wide,
Through every storm, I will abide.
In tempest's grip, I find my way,
A sturdy oak come break of day.

With roots so deep, I hold on tight,
In darkest hours, I seek the light.
No tempest fierce can tear apart,
The strength I bear, the warrior's heart.

So let the clouds collide and clash,
I rise anew from every crash.
Unyielding through the storm, I stand,
With courage forged by nature's hand.

Climbing Through Clouds

I rise on whispers of the wind,
Each step a promise, bright and thin.
Through wisp and shadow, I find my way,
Embracing dreams of light and play.

The summit glows with golden light,
While below, the world is lost from sight.
With every breath, I feel alive,
In this dance where hopes arrive.

The sky is vast, a canvas wide,
In clouds I see my fears subside.
The journey longs for joy to claim,
As I ascend, I shed my shame.

With arms stretched wide, I greet the air,
As I climb higher, heart laid bare.
The heights reveal what's deep inside,
In every heartbeat, a fierce pride.

Atop it all, I stand so firm,
Each gust of wind a joyful term.
In clouds I've found where I belong,
A symphony of hope and song.

Bone Deep Determination

With fire ignited in my core,
I face the trials, seek to explore.
Every obstacle fuels my quest,
Grind and grit put to the test.

The road is tough, the path unclear,
Yet every challenge draws me near.
With every fall, I learn to rise,
In struggle, strength wears no disguise.

Bone deep, the will I carry tight,
Through darkest hours, I chase the light.
Persistence flows inside my veins,
A fierce resolve that still remains.

Beyond the doubt, I forge ahead,
With every doubt, my spirit fed.
Though weary, still my heart beats strong,
In steadfast heart, I find my song.

For every scar that marks my skin,
A testament to what's within.
With bone deep courage, I shall stand,
Embracing life, with open hand.

Beneath the Weight of Wounds

Beneath the scars that tell my tale,
A silent strength begins to swell.
For every tear that traces skin,
A deeper wisdom waits within.

The wounds I carry, shadows cast,
Yet from their depths, my heart is vast.
In every ache, a chance to heal,
In silence, pain, I learn to feel.

The burden heavy, yet I rise,
With every breath, I touch the skies.
Resilience fuels my weary soul,
To mend the fractures, to be whole.

From ashes cold, I start anew,
With lessons learned from trials few.
The weight I bear, a badge of pride,
In pain's embrace, I won't abide.

Through every wound, my spirit grows,
Unfolding stories life bestows.
In twilight's glow, I find my grace,
Beneath the weight, I find my place.

Unbroken Spirit

In storms that rage and winds that howl,
I stand steadfast, refuse to cowl.
With every blow, the spirit soars,
Unbroken heart that seeks for more.

The trials test, the pressures bind,
Yet in my chest, a fire aligned.
I rise from ashes, fierce and bright,
With courage lit, I claim my light.

Through every fall, I learn to dance,
In every struggle, I find my chance.
With laughter ringing in the night,
The spirit thrives, a radiant sight.

Beyond the pain, I see the dawn,
In shadows cast, a strength is drawn.
With open arms, I greet the day,
A warrior spirit, come what may.

Forever strong, I'll face the tide,
With love and hope, my heart my guide.
An unbroken spirit sings so true,
In every moment, I'll renew.

Perseverance in Motion

With every step, I rise anew,
Chasing dreams in skies so blue.
The road is long, but I will go,
Through trials faced, my strength will grow.

I stumble, fall, then stand again,
The fire within, I'll not contain.
Each heartbeat drives me on my way,
For every night must yield to day.

Adversity, my driving force,
I'll navigate this winding course.
With grit and grace, I'll carve my path,
Finding peace amid the wrath.

Through stormy seas and winding roads,
I carry forth my heavy loads.
With every breath, I'll chase the sun,
Embracing battles yet unwon.

And when I feel I might just break,
I'll find the strength for hope's own sake.
For dreams are worth the price we pay,
In motion still, I'll forge my way.

From Ashes to Aspirations

From ashes cold, a fire ignites,
With dreams reborn, we reach new heights.
The past may haunt, yet hope remains,
In every loss, a lesson gains.

What once was lost, a chance to start,
With open hands and willing heart.
I'll rise again, unbowed, unbent,
This journey filled with pure intent.

In shadows deep, a flicker glows,
Amid the doubts, my vision grows.
From pain and struggle, strength I draw,
Redefining all I knew before.

Each breath in time, a step I take,
The road ahead, I'll not forsake.
Through trials faced, I craft my fate,
From ashes to my destined state.

With courage fierce, I'll face the flame,
From ashes raised, I'll stake my claim.
Inspiration drives my every move,
With heart and soul, each day I prove.

The Tenacity of Softness

In whispers low, I find my might,
A gentle heart that holds on tight.
With every tear, resilience blooms,
Softness thrives amid the glooms.

For strength resides in tender grace,
True courage wears a warm embrace.
In quiet moments, power grows,
A subtle force that always shows.

With open arms, I face the storm,
In vulnerability, I am warm.
For every bruise, a chance to heal,
The softest core, I choose to feel.

Though life may test my fragile will,
My spirit finds a way to fill.
With love and kindness as my guide,
In gentleness, I take my stride.

For tenacity, at times, is meek,
In softness lies the strength I seek.
With a quiet heart, I boldly stand,
And greet the world with open hand.

Strength Found in Shadows

In shadows deep, I find my might,
Where light is scarce, yet dreams ignite.
Through darkest nights, my spirit grows,
In silence found, the power flows.

With every trial, I learn to see,
That strength can rise from what may be.
In corners dark, the heart finds grace,
A spark of hope in every space.

Beneath the weight of shadows cast,
I'll unearth strength that's built to last.
In hidden realms, my courage blooms,
To find my way through silent dooms.

Embracing all that life can send,
In shadows deep, my fears will mend.
With every breath, I claim the night,
For even darkness brings its light.

From depths unknown, my heart takes flight,
With strength I gather, I face my plight.
In shadows, I will find my way,
A journey brightened by each day.

The Weight of Resilience

In shadows cast, we stand so tall,
With every stumble, we refuse to fall.
Through storms that rage, our spirits rise,
For in our hearts, the fire never dies.

Each challenge met, a lesson learned,
With every flame, we fiercely burned.
The weight we bear, a badge of pride,
In unity, our strength will abide.

We tread the path, though fraught with strife,
In the darkest hours, we find our life.
With courage wrapped in tender grace,
We lift each other, face to face.

Through whispered doubts, we forge ahead,
With every tear, new dreams are bred.
Our voices strong, a chorus of might,
Together, we embrace the fight.

So let us shine, through night and day,
Resilience guides us on our way.
With hearts entwined, we'll write our tale,
In every storm, we will prevail.

Starlight through the Ruins

Amid the wreckage, hope takes flight,
With starlit dreams to guide our sight.
In broken places, beauty grows,
With every dawn, the new light shows.

Through tangled vines and crumbled walls,
A gentle whisper, the universe calls.
Each shattered piece, a story told,
Of courage found, and hearts so bold.

The night unfolds its canvas wide,
Where shadows dance and fears collide.
Yet in the dark, we find our song,
A symphony where we belong.

Beneath the ruins, roots entwine,
In every fissure, life will shine.
Together we rise, with spirits bright,
Like constellations in the night.

So let the stars be our guiding light,
As we transcend the darkest height.
Starlight glimmers, a beacon clear,
Through the ruins, we'll conquer fear.

Threads of Hope Woven Deep

In every heart, a thread so fine,
Woven through struggles, intertwine.
A tapestry of dreams on display,
With colors bright, to guide our way.

Each moment steeped in gentle grace,
Uplifting spirits, a warm embrace.
Through trials faced, our courage shows,
As hope ignites, and kindness grows.

With hands held tight, we craft the weave,
In unity, we choose to believe.
Every stitch a promise made,
In shadows cast, our light won't fade.

Through every tear, a glimmer shines,
A testament of love that binds.
With threads of hope, our hearts will leap,
Together strong, our dreams wekeep.

As patterns form, our stories blend,
In every life, a chance to mend.
With visions clear and spirits steep,
We cherish all the threads we keep.

Illuminating the Unexpected

In the quiet moments, life unfolds,
With surprises that the heart beholds.
Through winding paths, the journey flows,
In every turn, a blossom grows.

When shadows loom and fears appear,
A spark ignites, dispelling fear.
Embrace the twist, the unknown thrill,
For in the chaos, we find our will.

The joy of serendipity sings,
Unlocking doors and unknown things.
With open hearts, we greet the chance,
As life invites us to a dance.

Each moment gifts a brand-new light,
Illuminating the path so bright.
From what was lost, a treasure found,
In unexpected, joy is unbound.

So let us wander, unafraid to roam,
In every surprise, we find our home.
With hearts that welcome what's anew,
We live each day, in vivid hue.

The Art of Letting Go

In shadows deep, the heart must tread,
Releasing dreams that once were fed.
With open hands, we find our peace,
Embracing change, our fears release.

The past, a whisper in the breeze,
No longer bound, we move with ease.
Each step unfolds a brand new dawn,
In letting go, our strength is drawn.

With every tear that stains the ground,
A space for growth can now be found.
We learn to trust the paths ahead,
In freedom's arms, our spirits spread.

For in the sorrow, wisdom grows,
A tapestry of highs and lows.
The art of letting go we know,
Is where our truest selves can glow.

Roots Firmly Planted

Deep in the earth, our roots entwine,
Strength in the soil, a bond divine.
Through storms and trials, we stand tall,
Nurtured by love, together we call.

Branches reach out, they stretch and thrive,
In sunlight's warmth, we feel alive.
Together we weather the fiercest storm,
With roots so strong, we stay warm.

The winds may howl, the shadows may creep,
Yet in our hearts, we hold our keep.
Firmly planted, we choose to rise,
Reaching for stars in the vast skies.

Within our core, resilience flows,
Through the challenges, our spirit glows.
With roots that dig, we face the day,
In unity's light, we find our way.

Weathered, Yet Whole

Each scar, a story, woven tight,
In every loss, there blooms new light.
With weathered hands, we carve our way,
Through life's wild dance, come what may.

The sun has shone, the rain has fell,
In every struggle, we learn to dwell.
Through tempest winds, our spirits soar,
Weathered, yet whole, we seek for more.

Like ancient trees bent but not broken,
We speak our truth without a token.
Resilience holds, though the years grow long,
In the symphony of life, we belong.

With every season, we fade and bloom,
Creating beauty amidst the gloom.
Weathered hearts, steadfast and bold,
In every chapter, our lives unfold.

Unmasking the Inner Warrior

Beneath the layers, the heart does fight,
A warrior stirs, awakening in light.
With courage ignited, we rise anew,
Unmask our fears and break through.

Each challenge faced, a battle won,
Strength flows deep like a river run.
In silence forged, we find our voice,
Embrace our power, rejoice, rejoice!

With every scar, our story grows,
Of fierce determination, the world knows.
Unyielding spirit, proud and free,
The warrior within is meant to be.

Through shadows cast, we stand our ground,
In unity's march, our hearts resound.
Unmasking strength, we forge the way,
For the inner warrior leads the day.

Cracked but Complete

In the mirror, a fractured view,
Pieces shimmer, a tale so true.
Though the cracks may tell their lore,
I stand resilient, forevermore.

Every scar, a story spun,
In the dance of life, I have won.
With each flaw, a beauty shines,
In the light where my spirit aligns.

Strength in silence, whispers bold,
Tales of warmth amidst the cold.
I gather fragments, each my own,
Cracked but whole, I have grown.

Through the tempest, I've learned to sway,
Finding peace in the fray.
In my heart, a gentle flame,
Cracked yet complete, I remain the same.

So here's to resilience, bright and clear,
In every echo, I hold dear.
With love, I stitch the past anew,
Cracked but complete, I rise and renew.

Courage in the Chaos

Amid the storm, I find my way,
In darkness, I'll choose to stay.
Holding tight to dreams at hand,
With courage strong, I make my stand.

Thunder roars, the shadows play,
Still I walk, come what may.
Each setback, a lesson learned,
In chaos, my spirit burned.

I gather strength from every fall,
In the tempest, I hear the call.
Waves may crash, but I won't drown,
With courage, I wear my crown.

The winds may howl, the skies may weep,
But in my heart, the promise I keep.
Chaos swirls like a raging sea,
Yet, within me, I am free.

So I dance through the storm's embrace,
With every step, I set my pace.
In the chaos, a fire inside,
With courage, I will always abide.

Echoes of a Stronger Self

In the silence, whispers rise,
Echoes dance beneath the skies.
From shadows deep, I seek the light,
A stronger self comes into sight.

Lessons learned, like grains of sand,
Shape my heart and steady my hand.
With every trial, I rise anew,
Echoes guide me, pure and true.

Through the valleys, beneath the stars,
I find my peace amidst the scars.
Every heartbeat a testament,
To a journey, fierce and heaven-sent.

I weave my past with threads of gold,
Creating strength from stories told.
Echoes linger, soft and kind,
A stronger self I now can find.

So here's to the echoes, loud and clear,
For every truth that I hold dear.
In the tapestry of life I weave,
Echoes of strength, I shall believe.

Heartfelt Reverberations

In the stillness of the night,
Hearts beat softly, pure delight.
Each rhythm holds a story told,
In heartfelt warmth, we break the mold.

With every pulse, the world aligns,
In gentle whispers, love defines.
From every tear, a rainbow forms,
Heartfelt echoes through the storms.

Together we rise, entwined as one,
Finding strength, the journey's begun.
In laughter's light, and sorrow's shade,
Heartfelt reverberations are made.

Each moment shared, a treasure bright,
In the tapestry of endless night.
With every heartbeat, dreams ignite,
In heartfelt songs, we take flight.

So here we are, through thick and thin,
In every loss, we still can win.
With reverberations that forever last,
Hearts intertwined, a steadfast cast.

The Light that Endures

In shadows deep, a soft glow shines,
Guiding hearts through heavy vines.
A spark that warms the coldest night,
A beacon bright, forever light.

Through storms that rage and winds that howl,
The light remains, a steady prowl.
With every step, it leads the way,
A promise of hope at break of day.

When doubt descends like thickened fog,
It pierces through, a faithful log.
In every heart, its flame resides,
A truth that swells and never hides.

Time may wear, but light stays strong,
A melody in life's great song.
It whispers tales of those who dream,
And nurtures all with gentle gleam.

So heed the glow, let it inspire,
To rise anew, to reach higher.
For in the dark, it finds a way,
To spark the dawn of a brand new day.

Resilient Echoes

In the silence, whispers call,
The echoes rise, they never fall.
Stories wrapped in wings of time,
Resilient voices, bold in rhyme.

Through valleys deep and mountains high,
They teach us how to laugh and cry.
Each lesson learned, a gentle push,
To face the world, to never hush.

Though obstacles may block the view,
Echoes remind us of what's true.
With every stumble, we find the grace,
To stand upright, to embrace our place.

In every heartbeat, every sigh,
A testament that we can fly.
Resilient souls, with courage bright,
Carving paths through endless night.

So in the quiet, listen close,
To echoes that inspire the most.
Their strength is what we all can share,
A symphony of love and care.

A Canvas of Resolve

Upon the canvas, dreams unfold,
In vibrant hues, both warm and bold.
Each brushstroke tells a tale profound,
A masterpiece from heart unbound.

With colors bright, we paint our fate,
Embracing storms, we challenge hate.
With every layer, hope appears,
Transforming pain into our cheers.

From shadows cast to light embraced,
We forge ahead, with love we're laced.
A tapestry of strength and grace,
In unity, we find our place.

The canvas shifts, but will not break,
A resolve strong, no fear to take.
As life unfolds its wondrous art,
We hold the brush, we play our part.

So let us paint with all our might,
A vision born from darkest night.
For in our hearts, we hold the key,
To a canvas bright, a life set free.

Threads of Grace

In gentle weaves, the threads entwine,
Each fiber tells a story fine.
Through tangled paths and woven dreams,
A tapestry of life redeems.

With every stitch, a bond is formed,
In humble hearts, compassion warmed.
The seams of joy and sorrow blend,
Creating gifts that never end.

In colors rich, the fabric flows,
Of laughter shared, of tears that glow.
Each thread reflects, a journey shared,
In grace, we rise, in love declared.

Through trials faced, we find the way,
To lift each other day by day.
With threads of hope, we weave anew,
In every heart, the strength shines through.

As pieces fall, we stitch again,
In unity, we conquer pain.
With threads of grace, we craft our fate,
Together strong, we celebrate.

Shadows of Resilience

In the twilight, hope remains,
Whispers of dreams in quiet lanes.
Through storms that echo like lost chimes,
We find our strength in silent rhymes.

Footsteps echo on these paths,
Guided by light, we face the wrath.
Through valleys deep and mountains steep,
The soul awakens from its sleep.

Heavy hearts bear stories old,
Woven in courage, brave and bold.
With every tear, a seed is sown,
In harshest soils, the truth is grown.

Fading shadows dance in grace,
Emboldened spirits, we embrace.
The twilight banishes despair,
For in the dark, we find our air.

Harness the scars, let them show,
Each mark a seed for what will grow.
In unity, we rise anew,
Shadows of strength, forever true.

Unyielding Hearts

Wars are fought in silence deep,
Unyielding hearts, their promises keep.
Fires burn with fervent might,
In darkest hours, we seek the light.

Chains may bind, but spirits soar,
Resilient souls, we rise for more.
With every challenge that we face,
We carve our dreams, we find our place.

Together we stand, hand in hand,
In every struggle, united we band.
Voices rise above the strife,
Unyielding hearts, the pulse of life.

Through the storms and raging tide,
Hope remains, our constant guide.
With every bruise, a victory claimed,
In the quiet, our love is famed.

When the world tries to bring us low,
Unyielding hearts will fiercely glow.
With every heartbeat, every breath,
We conquer doubt, embrace the depth.

The Beauty in Scars

Each scar tells a tale untold,
A story of strength, brave and bold.
In every line, a victory sung,
The beauty of life, forever young.

Wounds may fade, but lessons last,
With every shadow, we shed the past.
A tapestry rich with colors bright,
Hearts emerge from the darkest night.

In the mirror, we see the art,
Crafted by time, the pulse of heart.
Embracing flaws, we wear them proud,
A symphony whispered, no need for loud.

Through raging storms and raging seas,
We seek the calm, the gentle breeze.
In every heartbeat, every sigh,
We rise above, letting fears die.

The beauty in scars, a precious gem,
In every fissure, a chance to stem.
A reminder of battles, love, and grace,
In every mark, we find our place.

Rising from Ashes

From ashes deep, a whisper grows,
A phoenix born where sorrow flows.
Silhouettes dance in twilight's glow,
Embers spark as spirits know.

Through fires that once brought us low,
We gather strength, let courage show.
With wings unfurled and hearts ablaze,
We face the dawn, we greet the days.

Resilience found in shattered dreams,
We stitch the fragments with hopeful seams.
In darkness, light begins to weave,
A tapestry rich, of those who believe.

Rising from ashes, we reclaim the night,
With every breath, we rise to fight.
Together we soar, the past takes flight,
In love's embrace, we find our light.

So here we stand, reborn anew,
With scars and strength, we will break through.
In every heartbeat, every sigh,
Rising from ashes, we touch the sky.

Resilient Shadows

In the light where shadows play,
They dance but never fade away.
Whispers of hope in the night,
Carving paths toward the light.

Through storms that shake the ground,
In silence, strength is found.
Each step, a story to unfold,
Resilience written bold.

Beyond the clouds, the sun will rise,
With every tear, a new surprise.
They've worn the weight of time's embrace,
But shadows find their place.

A heart beats fiercely in the dark,
Lighting flames with every spark.
From ashes, dreams begin to soar,
Resilient shadows evermore.

Weathered Heartstrings

Strings that pull, that bind and break,
In tunes of loss, the heart does ache.
Every note a tale to tell,
Of storms that raged, yet we still dwell.

Weathered paths, we walk alone,
Yet in our hearts, the seeds are sown.
Harmony in the disarray,
Finding strength in every sway.

The laughter and the sorrow blend,
With every chapter, we ascend.
Tattered notes in life's refrain,
Weathered heartstrings feel the pain.

But in the struggle, melodies grow,
Resilience in every low.
With every strum, the heart takes flight,
Weathered strings will shine so bright.

The Strength of Scars

Each scar a map, a story told,
Of fierce battles, brave and bold.
In the depths of pain, we find,
The strength of scars, intertwined.

Shadows linger, memories burn,
But from the wounds, we always learn.
With each reminder, our spirits rise,
The strength of scars, our greatest prize.

Transformed by trials, we stand tall,
With every stumble, we hear the call.
Embracing flaws, we wear them proud,
The strength of scars, our hearts unbowed.

Through the valleys, we will tread,
Carrying stories of courage spread.
In vulnerability, we see the art,
The strength of scars, a work of heart.

Echoes of Endurance

In the silence, echoes ring,
Whispers of the pain we bring.
Lessons learned from each fall,
The echoes of endurance call.

Through the trials, a voice remains,
Resilience flows through all the pains.
With every challenge, we embrace,
Echoes of strength, time won't erase.

The heart beats on, fierce and free,
Navigating through the debris.
In shadows cast, we stand our ground,
Echoes of endurance, profound.

Worn and weary, still we strive,
In the depths, we feel alive.
With every breath, a tribute sings,
Echoes of endurance take their wings.

The Underbelly of Strength

In shadows deep, where few have tread,
The weight of worlds rests on hearts,
Silent struggles, courage spread,
Hidden battles, where hope imparts.

Beneath the surface, quiet grows,
The will to rise, though feeling low,
Strength forged in pain, the river flows,
A force unseen, its power glows.

Whispers of doubt in evening's tide,
Yet dreams persist, undying light,
Through darkest nights, a spark inside,
Emerging strong, they rise in flight.

The weight of chains, a heavy load,
Yet every step, a journey starts,
A testament to unheard road,
Where strength resides within our hearts.

So here we stand, though weary, worn,
In every crack, the deep-rooted rise,
Out of despair, the soul reborn,
In unity, we claim the skies.

A Song of Persevering Souls

Through tempest winds, they forge ahead,
With grit and grace, they face the storm,
Each heavy step, like words unsaid,
Their song of hope, a timeless norm.

In shadows cast, they find their way,
With every fall, they learn to stand,
The heart persists, come what may,
Together strong, they make their band.

Voices blend, a symphony sweet,
In every note, a tale unfolds,
Beneath the struggle, triumph meets,
In unity, their story molds.

With every tear, a lesson learned,
In every challenge, strength is drawn,
Through fires faced, their spirits burned,
A brighter dawn, they always spawn.

So sing their song, both loud and clear,
For hearts that walk the road unknown,
In every pulse, their dreams adhere,
The song of souls, forever grown.

Battered Wings Still Soar

With battered wings, they learn to fly,
Although the storms have tried their best,
They rise above, touch the sky,
In trials faced, they find their rest.

Through broken dreams, they find the way,
A dance of hope, a gentle breeze,
Each soar and dip, a bold display,
In resilience, they learn to seize.

The scars of battles, etched in grace,
Each gust of wind, a guiding force,
With every struggle, they embrace,
A journey carved, a steadfast course.

In the quiet spaces, strength reclaims,
Every falter, a lesson's seed,
In every heart, the fire flames,
They forge ahead, enriched by need.

So let them soar, though wings may shake,
For in their flight, the spirit aims,
Through trials faced, the world they shake,
In battered wings, the brave proclaim.

Resilience Remembers

In echoes soft, the past endures,
Resilience marks each step we take,
Carved in the soul where hope ensures,
The strength to rise, no fear to break.

We carry tales of joy and pain,
In every heartbeat, stories weave,
Though storms have passed and left their stain,
A tapestry, we still believe.

Through tears and laughter, shadows blend,
In every note, our voices ring,
The heart's resilience, never bends,
From ashes, life begins to spring.

In quiet moments, truth recalls,
The battles fought, the victories won,
Through ancient trials, our spirit calls,
In every dawn, we rise as one.

So cherish what the past imparts,
For every fall has made us strong,
In unity, with open hearts,
Resilience sings our lasting song.

In the Wake of Struggles

In the depths of night, we stand so tall,
Facing fears that echo, yet we won't fall.
Through storms and shadows, we trace our path,
Finding strength in the aftermath.

Each challenge a lesson, each tear a spark,
Igniting the fire that burns in the dark.
With hearts intertwined, we find our way,
Emerging brighter, come what may.

The weight of the world rests on weary backs,
But hope is the compass, guiding off tracks.
In unity we rise, as we share the load,
Together we conquer, together we've strode.

Beneath the ruins, new dreams ignite,
Building our futures from the remnants of night.
With every heartbeat, we carve our fate,
In the wake of struggles, we create.

So let the winds howl, let the tides crash,
We will not falter, we will not thrash.
In the light of dawn, shadows will flee,
In the wake of struggles, we shall be free.

Embracing the Cracks

In the porcelain world, we find our way,
Embracing the flaws, come what may.
The lines of our stories, etched in gold,
Reveal the beauty in paths once untold.

Each imperfection, a note in our song,
Teaching us where we truly belong.
Through the broken places, light pours in,
Transforming our boundaries, where we begin.

In the cracks, we plant seeds of grace,
Finding sanctuary in every space.
With open hearts, we gather the shards,
Reclaiming our power, not playing our cards.

A tapestry woven from joy and pain,
In the sunshine and the rain.
With every fracture, we learn to mend,
In embracing the cracks, we transcend.

A mosaic of laughter, a canvas of tears,
Weaving connections through all of our fears.
In each little gap, beauty unwinds,
Embracing the cracks, we redefine.

Weathered Wings

Worn by the tempests, sturdy and wise,
Weathered wings whisper under vast skies.
With every gust, they learn to glide,
Carrying stories that swell with pride.

Through darkened clouds and lonesome nights,
They dance with the stars, pursuing the lights.
Each flap, a promise, each glide, a gift,
In the heart of the storm, they find their lift.

Horizon beckons, adventures await,
With dreams woven tightly, they navigate fate.
Over mountains and valleys, they soar so high,
Weathered wings painting the canvas of sky.

In the grace of the winds, freedom takes flight,
Unburdened by doubt, they chase the light.
A testament carved by trials they've seen,
Weathered wings blossom, forever serene.

As dawn breaks anew, they stretch out their span,
Embodying courage in every plan.
With each passing moment, they rise and sing,
In the embrace of the heavens, weathered wings.

The Power of Stillness

In the hush of the dawn, where whispers meet,
Lies the power of stillness, soft and sweet.
Time slows its march, in tranquil embrace,
Embracing the silence, we find our place.

In the stillness, voices of wisdom arise,
Echoing softly, like tender sighs.
The chaos may pulse, but here we reside,
Finding strength in the calm, with hearts open wide.

Moments of solitude reveal the truth,
In the quiet, we nurture our youth.
A breath, a thought, the world fades away,
In the power of stillness, we learn to stay.

The dance of the leaves, the flutter of wings,
Each pause a reminder of simple things.
In the beauty of silence, we gather our might,
Facing life's battles, igniting our light.

So let the world bustle, let it roar and run,
In our hearts, the stillness has finally won.
With open arms and serene hearts, we gleam,
In the power of stillness, we dare to dream.

Wounds that Speak

In shadows cast by silent pain,
The echoes tell what's hard to feign.
With scars that map a troubled past,
A story woven deep and vast.

Each tear that fell, a tale untold,
Of battles fought, and dreams turned cold.
Yet in the depths of darkest night,
A spark ignites, a flickering light.

The heart, a canvas bruised and torn,
Holds beauty in the ways it's worn.
For wounds can speak, their voices clear,
A symphony of hope and fear.

Through whispers soft, the truths arise,
Each hurt a thread, under the skies.
Together stitched, they paint the soul,
A testament, a journey whole.

So let the scars be badges bright,
A sign of strength that weathered fight.
For every wound that speaks with grace,
Becomes a part of our embrace.

Trials of a Brave Heart

In the stillness, courage brews,
A heart that dares, a spirit true.
Across the valleys, steep and wide,
Brave souls march on, with hope as guide.

Each trial faced, a lesson learned,
Through fires stoked, the fortitude burned.
With every step, the ground may shake,
Yet still they rise, no fear to break.

When shadows loom and doubts reside,
The brave heart stands, refuses to hide.
With steadfast will, they pierce the gloom,
Transforming fears into heart's bloom.

The journey steep, the path unclear,
Yet every stumble, they persevere.
With grit and grace, they face the storm,
Emerging strong, in new form born.

Trials may test, but never bend,
A heart so brave will surely mend.
For every challenge, they impart,
A spark of hope, a beating heart.

A Tapestry of Triumph

In the loom of life, threads intertwine,
Each shade a journey, unique design.
With colors bright and edges rough,
A tapestry forms, both tender and tough.

Moments of joy, and those of grief,
Weaved with purpose, a shared belief.
From laughter's echo to sorrow's sigh,
The fabric tells of the reasons why.

Strength is found in the fibers spun,
Within the struggles, victories won.
Every knot holds a tale untold,
A testament to the brave and bold.

As patterns shift, and stories blend,
A rich mosaic of hearts they send.
Embroidered dreams and hopes so grand,
Together they rise, hand in hand.

So cherish each thread, each hue and line,
For in this tapestry, we all shine.
A story woven, proud and free,
A legacy of you and me.

The Strength Beneath the Surface

Beneath the calm, a tempest brews,
Hidden depths, with strength imbues.
Like quiet roots that grip the ground,
An unseen force, profound, unbound.

When waves of doubt crash on the shore,
The steadfast heart will still explore.
For in the silence, power grows,
A quiet strength only one knows.

Through every trial, each stormy night,
Resilience shines, an inner light.
With every struggle faced alone,
The strength beneath reveals its own.

Like mountains standing tall and proud,
They weather storms, and break the cloud.
The Echoes of their steadfast core,
A symphony of strength and more.

So when the world may seem unfair,
And burdens heavy, hard to bear,
Remember this, the truth profound,
Your strength beneath will know no bound.

Fortitude Against the Odds

In shadows deep, we stand tall,
With hopes that never fall.
Each challenge faced, we rise strong,
Resilience hums our life-long song.

Against the storm, we find our way,
Through darkest night to break of day.
A spirit fierce, unyielding, bright,
We keep our dreams within our sight.

Though walls may close and fears may creep,
Our will is strong, our faith is deep.
With every step, we claim our ground,
In silent strength, our strength is found.

We gather hope from scattered seeds,
In every heart, a fire feeds.
From ashes rise, we dare to tread,
With courage bold, our path is spread.

So let the odds come crashing in,
Our hearts ignited, we begin.
For every wound, a story told,
In fortitude, we shine like gold.

Hearts Like Armor

With hearts like armor, strong and bright,
   We face the battles, day and night.
   Each scar a mark, each tear a tale,
     In unity, we shall prevail.

Through trials fierce, we hold our ground,
In whispered strength, our hope is found.
   Together bound, we rise, we stand,
   In every challenge, hand in hand.

The world may shake, but we won't yield,
   In faith and love, we've got a shield.
   Our spirits soar, unbent, unbowed,
   For in our hearts, the brave are loud.

   We weather storms, we face the heat,
  With hearts as one, we feel complete.
    To every struggle, we respond,
    In strength united, we absorb.

So let them come, with all their might,
   For together, we'll seek the light.
  In every struggle, we find our way,
With hearts like armor, come what may.

Through the Valley of Trials

Through the valley, shadows loom,
Yet in our hearts, we find our bloom.
With every challenge, courage grows,
In every step, compassion flows.

The path may twist, the road may bend,
Yet on this journey, there's no end.
With eyes wide open, we embrace,
The trials weave a sacred space.

In whispers soft, the truth will speak,
Through every struggle, we grow meek.
From fear, we shape a brighter dream,
In unity, together we seem.

Each burden shared, a lighter load,
In every heart, a journey owed.
Through valleys vast, we lean on love,
Guided by stars that shine above.

So onward through the winds we sway,
With steadfast hearts, we light the way.
For in our trials, we find our voice,
In every challenge, we rejoice.

Silent Battles

In silent battles, shadows fight,
With whispered dreams in the night.
Our struggles hide beneath the skin,
Yet in our souls, the wars begin.

Each day we rise, the world to face,
In quiet strength, we find our place.
Through every tear and every sigh,
We stand as one, we reach for sky.

Though silent cries may fill the air,
In every heart, a sacred prayer.
With every breath a choice we make,
In endless love, our spirits wake.

We fight for hope, we fight for peace,
With every battle, we find release.
Through darkened paths our light will guide,
In silent battles, love won't hide.

So whisper soft, and hold on tight,
Together we shall face the night.
Amidst the clang, the chaos loud,
In silent battles, we walk proud.

Loud Victories

With loud victories, our hearts soar high,
In every triumph, we touch the sky.
Together we dance, our spirits free,
In every win, our unity.

The cheers resound, in joy we sing,
For every challenge, we found our wings.
Through trials faced and battles won,
We hold our heads high, like the sun.

With open arms, we greet the day,
In light of love, we find our way.
With every step, our laughter rings,
In loud victories, our spirit sings.

So gather round, and raise a toast,
To every moment, we cherish most.
Together still, through thick and thin,
With loud victories, we begin.

In joy, we rise, in love we trust,
With every heartbeat, our hearts combust.
In unity's name, we claim our fate,
In loud victories, we celebrate.

Shattered Yet Shining

In pieces I lay, a canvas of light,
With fragments that glimmer, a haunting sight.
Each shard tells a story, a silent scream,
Yet through the darkness, I dare to dream.

Though scars may linger, they weave a tale,
Of battles fought fiercely, of courage unveiled.
I gather the remnants, with trembling hands,
And craft a mosaic where hope still stands.

The light breaks through, in a dazzling embrace,
A reminder that beauty can rise from disgrace.
Shattered yet shining, I learn to be free,
Embracing the chaos, the strength that's in me.

With each dawning sun, I rise to reclaim,
The dreams once lost in a flickering flame.
I am not defeated, but forged anew,
In every reflection, my power shines through.

So here I stand, with my heart open wide,
Embracing the journey, my faith as my guide.
For in every fracture, there's light to refine,
A spirit unbroken, forever divine.

The Will to Carry On

When shadows loom large, and hope feels far,
I gather my strength beneath a midnight star.
With each heavy heartbeat, I find my way,
Through the tempest of sorrow, I'll seize the day.

The road may be rocky, each step a test,
But deep in my soul, I know I am blessed.
For every small triumph, each whisper of grace,
Reminds me of courage that time won't erase.

In moments of doubt, I'll hold tight to dreams,
For they are the lifelines that flicker and gleam.
In the depth of the struggle, I'll learn to be strong,
With the will to carry on, I'll right every wrong.

With the dawn of each day, I'll rise and stand tall,
Embracing the journey, I'll never let fall.
Each challenge I face is a stepping stone,
For in the fight forward, I find I'm not alone.

So here I shall journey, with hope in my heart,
Every path that I take is a work of art.
With resilience ignited, I'll craft my own song,
For the will to carry on is forever strong.

Resilience in Every Breath

In whispers of wind, I find my refrain,
Each breath a reminder, a dance through the pain.
With every exhale, the burdens I shed,
Resilience blossoms where fear once tread.

When storms rage around, and doubts start to creep,
I anchor my soul in the promises deep.
In the cradle of stillness, I learn to embrace,
The power of patience, the gift of this space.

In moments of struggle, I'll rise from the ash,
Rebirth in my spirit, a fierce, shining flash.
For life's woven tapestry is rich and vast,
Every thread of resilience helps me hold fast.

Through valleys of shadows, I'll carry my light,
For darkness is fleeting, and hope is my sight.
With each tiny heartbeat, I strengthen the flame,
Resilience in every breath, I'll rise just the same.

So here I breathe deeply, the world all around,
With courage unyielding, on solid ground.
In the tapestry woven, I find my own strength,
Resilience in every breath, at any length.

Threads of Tenacity

In the loom of my heart, resilience is spun,
Each thread a reminder that I am not done.
With colors of courage, I weave and I mend,
Threads of tenacity that never shall bend.

Through trials and troubles, I gather my might,
In shadows, I find that I can still fight.
With every strong fiber, a story unfolds,
Of battles and victories, of courage retold.

In the fabric of life, I'm stitched with a dream,
A quilt of connection, where hope is the seam.
Though storms may try to unravel my path,
The threads of tenacity withstand every wrath.

As seasons keep changing, I learn to embrace,
The beauty in struggle, the strength in the grace.
For woven together, we rise and we sing,
Threads of tenacity in every small thing.

So here I will stand, with my heart open wide,
Weaving a tapestry where faith is my guide.
Each thread that I cherish, a link in my chain,
Threads of tenacity, forever remain.

The Light Through the Veil

A soft glow breaks the dawn,
Whispers flicker in the air.
Shadows dance, slowly withdrawn,
Hope emerges from despair.

As the mist begins to clear,
Gentle beams touch fragile ground.
Every heartbeat, loud and near,
In the quiet, peace is found.

Nature's promise softly calls,
Emerging blooms greet the light.
Through the cracks the beauty sprawls,
Filling darkness with delight.

With each ray, the world ignites,
Colors blend in vibrant hues.
In the chaos, calm ignites,
A reminder: we choose.

So we journey, hand in hand,
Through the veils of night and day.
Finding strength on shifting sand,
As the light shows us the way.

Surviving the Storm

The winds howl, fierce and loud,
Branches bend and leaves take flight.
In the tempest, we are bowed,
Yet we stand with all our might.

The clouds pour their heavy tears,
Lightning splits the sky in two.
Through the chaos, face your fears,
Hold your ground, and see it through.

Raindrops dance on the pavement,
Each one tells a tale of fight.
Survival is a testament,
To the strength within our sight.

As the storm begins to fade,
Colors bloom in morning light.
From the battles that we wade,
Emerges hope, a pure delight.

We are forged in nature's fire,
Resilience wrapped in our skin.
Facing every dark desire,
With the courage deep within.

Whispers of Hope

In the silence, voices dwell,
Softly echoing the dreams.
Tales of love and tales to tell,
In the heart where hope redeems.

Stars alight in endless night,
Guiding souls through shadows deep.
In the dark, we seek the bright,
Sowing seeds of faith to keep.

Paths once lost can be regained,
Footsteps light on paths anew.
Through the struggle, we have gained,
Strength in bonds that pull us through.

When the world feels cold and stark,
Gentle breezes brush our skin.
In the dawn, we find the spark,
Whispers tell us to begin.

So let the whispers take their flight,
Carried on the wings of time.
Every heartbeat, pure and bright,
Tells a story, sweet as rhyme.

Grit Beneath the Skin

There's a fire in my veins,
Burning bright with every scar.
Lessons learned through joys and pains,
Guiding me to rise and spar.

Silent battles, fought within,
Strengthened by each fall I've known.
In the struggle, I begin,
Finding grit that's mine alone.

Every setback, every strain,
Fuels the passion in my soul.
Through the hurt, I feel no pain,
For in trials, I find my whole.

With each breath, I stand defiant,
Facing storms that life has spun.
In the chaos, there's a quiet,
Where the strongest hearts are won.

I embrace the way I'm made,
Standing tall with roots that run.
In the shadows, hope cascades,
Shining bright, though battle's done.

The Courage to Rise

In shadows deep, where fears reside,
A flicker gleams, a heart's soft guide.
With trembling hands and eyes aglow,
We gather strength to face the foe.

The mountain looms, yet we will climb,
Through storms that roar and mountains prime.
Each step we take, we claim our space,
The courage blooms; we find our pace.

Though doubt may whisper, hope will shout,
With every breath, we push the doubt.
For in our souls, the fire ignites,
We stand as one, embracing heights.

With every bruise, we learn to stand,
In unity, we join a band.
Through trials faced, we stand in grace,
Together we rise, a warm embrace.

So let the world throw all it can,
In steel we stand, in heart, a plan.
For every fall will teach us well,
With courage fierce, we'll break the spell.

Unshattered Dreams

In quiet nights, dreams softly brew,
Whispers of hope, in hearts so true.
Each star above holds stories tight,
Of paths untraveled, endless light.

With every breath, we paint our skies,
Unfurling wings, where spirit flies.
Though storms may come and shadows loom,
We hold our dreams, like flowers bloom.

In gentle hands, the visions grow,
Through every trial, we learn to flow.
The heart beats loud, persistent song,
In every moment, we belong.

With laughter bright, we chase the dawn,
Renewing strength, as fears are gone.
Together we weave, a tapestry,
Of unshattered dreams, wild and free.

So let us sing, let voices soar,
For every dream opens a door.
With courage strong, we take our stand,
Unshattered dreams, a future planned.

Healing in the Aftermath

After the storm, the silence speaks,
In whispered tones, the heart still seeks.
The wounds may ache, but time reveals,
A path to peace, the spirit heals.

With every tear, a lesson learned,
In ashes cold, a fire is burned.
From brokenness, we start anew,
A journey deep, where hope shines through.

The sun will rise, dispelling night,
In these shadows, we find the light.
With every breath, we claim our strength,
In healing hands, we travel length.

Through whispered prayers, we start to mend,
The ties of love that never end.
In gentle moments, we embrace,
The beauty born from time and space.

So let the past give way to shine,
In every scar, a story fine.
With open hearts, we find our path,
In healing grace, we craft our wrath.

Silent Victories

In quiet hours, victories unfold,
In whispered truths, brave hearts are bold.
With every step, a journey slow,
We gather strength in what we know.

No roaring crowds, no cheers aloud,
Yet still we rise, through unseen shroud.
For every smile hides battles fought,
In silent wins, our dreams are caught.

When chaos rules, we find our peace,
In stillness, we embrace release.
With courage built, our spirits soar,
Each quiet win opens a door.

Through darkest nights, we hold the flame,
In every heart, we share the same.
No medals worn to show our fight,
In silent victories, we find our light.

So let us cherish the paths we pave,
In quiet moments, strong and brave.
For every win that stays unseen,
Is where we find what brave can mean.

Milton Keynes UK
Ingram Content Group UK Ltd.
UKHW021629011224
451755UK00010B/533